I0213469

JANE GOODALL'S ANIMAL WORLD

HIPPOS

by Miriam Schlein

Scientific Consultant: Alan Root

Photographs by Leonard Lee Rue III and Len Rue, Jr.

A Byron Preiss Book

iBooks for Young Readers

Habent Sua Fata Libelli

◇ Introduction: The Hippopotamus by Jane Goodall

The first hippopotamus I saw in the wild was when I was on a small boat on Lake Victoria, that huge stretch of water that is surrounded by Tanzania, Uganda and Kenya. We had anchored for the night—myself and my mother and two African crew. The sun had just set and the evening was quiet and beautiful. Suddenly there was a swirling sound in the water—and there, just a few yards away, was the head of a hippo. I think it must have been a male—a bull as they are called—for it was such an enormous head. Before darkness fell other hippos had appeared. They watched us for a while, from their strange pink-rimmed eyes, then slowly submerged. All that night we were serenaded by their extraordinary grunting, honk-honk-honk sounds. Our captain did not much like them so close. Hippos are thought to be one of the most dangerous animals in Africa, killing many people each year. Hippos are territorial, and sometimes they seem to hate small boats coming into their territorial water.

My most amazing encounter with a hippo was one night when I was taking a walk along the beach in Dar es Salaam. It was very dark, and it was only when I turned my flashlight on that I could see that the large creature that appeared to be rushing towards me from the sea was actually a hippo. Hippos are freshwater creatures—my hippo must have been a young bull, turned out of his herd, and moving along the sea shore in search of another river where he could set up a family of his own. I often wonder what happened to him because, as is the case in all parts of the hippos' range in Africa, there was not really anywhere left for him to go—humans are living in the places where, even twenty years ago, he could have found a new home with others of his kind.

In this book you will learn more about the hippo. Only by studying this fascinating creature can we hope to help save its habitat and preserve the way it lives in the wild.

◇ Contents

◇ Where Do Hippos Live?

About 2 million years ago hippos could be found in Africa, Europe, and Asia. In fact, hippos still existed in Europe until about 11,000 years ago. They lived in Asia until only a few hundred years ago. And they disappeared in Northern Africa when people took over their living space for farms and hunted them to extinction.

Today hippos live in large areas of south and central Africa, near rivers and lakes. Days, they spend in the water, resting. At night, they come up on land to eat grass. This is why they have the scientific name *Hippopotamus amphibius*. "Hippopotamus" means "river horse" in Greek. "Amphibious" means "able to live on land and in water." Often we shorten the name and just say "hippo."

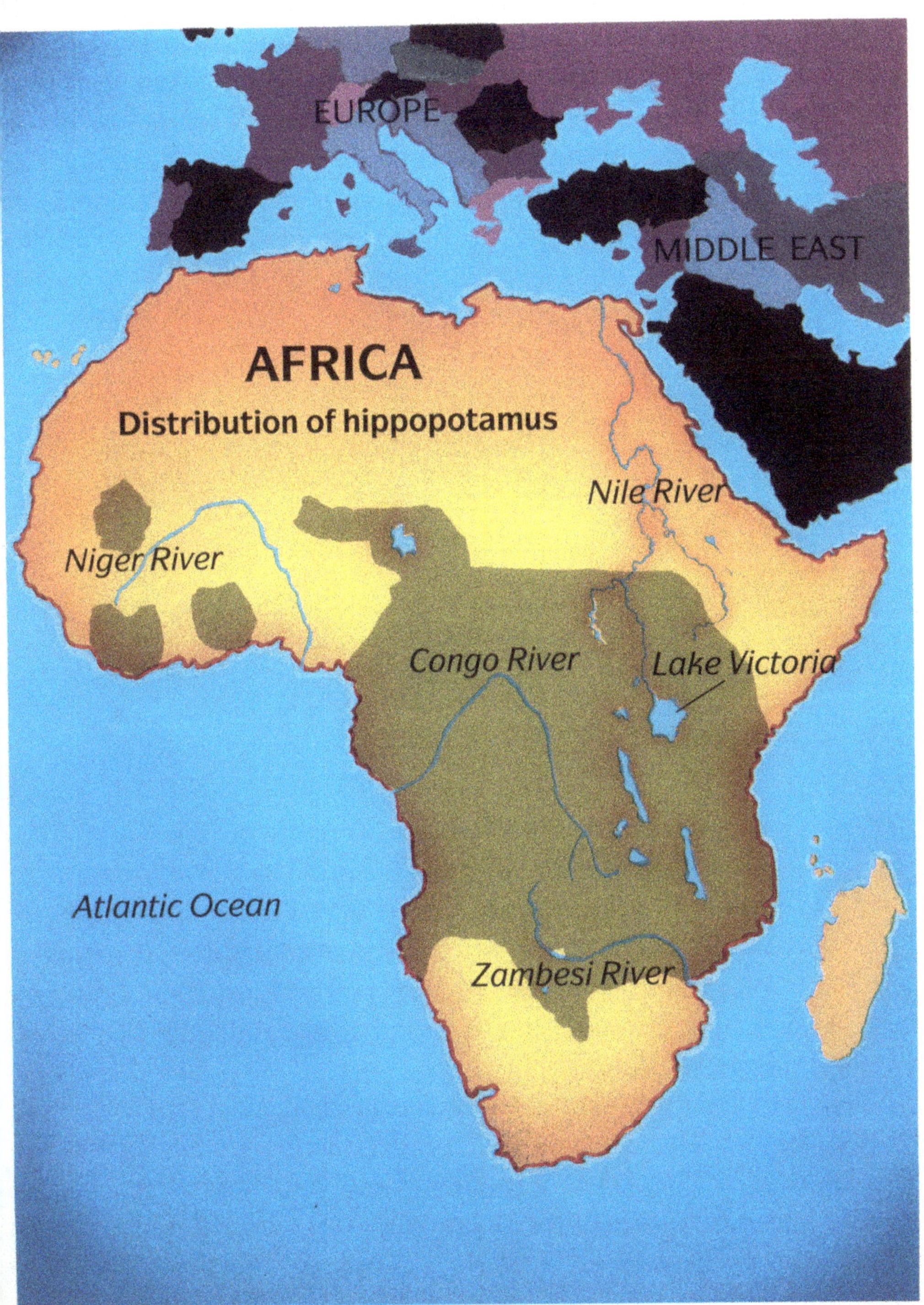
EUROPE
MIDDLE EAST
AFRICA
Distribution of hippopotamus
Nile River
Niger River
Congo River
Lake Victoria
Atlantic Ocean
Zambesi River

◇ The Family Tree of the Hippo

Scientists called taxonomists classify animals into groups, depending on the traits they share. The hippo is one kind of animal that scientists group under the name *artiodactyl* (ar-tee-oh-*dack*-till). These are the hoofed mammals that have an even number of toes. All artiodactyls are *herbivores*, or plant-eaters. Some other artiodactyls are pigs, goats, giraffes, deer, and camels.

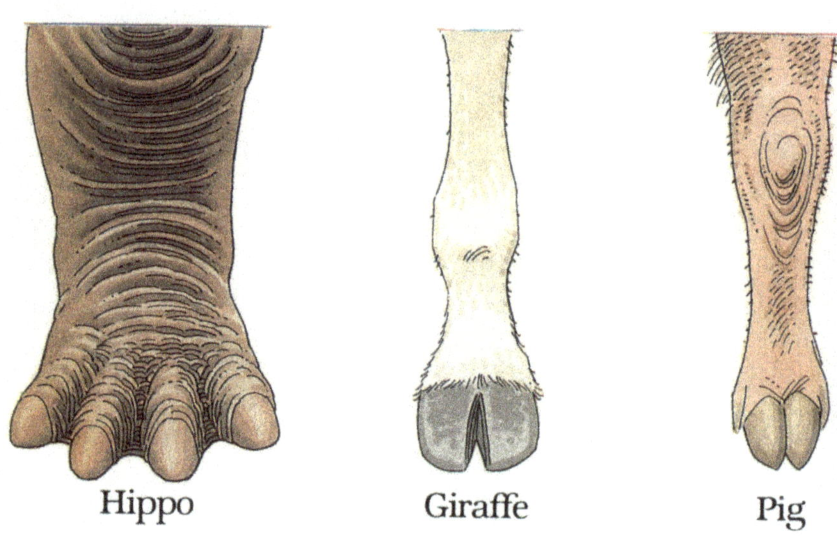

Hippo Giraffe Pig

The first artiodactyls lived about 30 million years ago. One group of these early piglike animals is called *anthracotheres* (*an*-thruh-koh-theers). Like hippos, they lived in lakes and rivers.

The *Bothriodon* (*both*-ree-o-don) was one of these. It looked a lot like a hippo, except its snout was pointed, and its eyes were not as high on its head. It is from this animal that the hippo evolved, about 4 million years ago.

Today there are two species, or types, of hippos. One is the big "river" hippo. The other is the smaller, rarer species called the pygmy hippo. This book is mainly about the river hippo.

The scientific name of the pygmy hippo is *Choeropsis liberiensis* (chuh-*rop*-sis lie-*beer*-ee-en-sis): "piglike, of Liberia." They live

This is the evolutionary family tree of the hippo. Today's animals are depicted on the top branches of the tree.

deep in the forests of western Africa, near swampy mud wallows. They sleep by day and wander at night, eating grass, leaves, and fruit. Unlike the river hippo, pygmy hippos live in pairs or alone.

◇ The Hippo Community

River hippos are social animals. They usually live in groups of ten, twenty, or more. Some groups have numbered more than 100. The females and young hippos stay together in a group called a *nursery*.

The adult male hippos stay around the edge of the nursery. Each one has his own special *territory* staked out. When one male moves into another's territory, a fight can begin. They slash at each other with their long, curved teeth. Many male hippos have

big scars on their bodies from these fights. Sometimes they even kill each other.

When a male hippo is grown enough to move out of the nursery, he first takes a spot on the outskirts of the group. Over time he has to fight his way into a territory closer to the females. There, he will have a better chance to mate with a female hippo.

◇ Sizing Up the Hippo

In weight, the hippo is the second largest land mammal. Elephants are the biggest. In body size, the hippo is the third biggest land mammal. A white rhino can be larger, but weighs less than a hippo.

The biggest mammal of all, the blue whale, lives in the sea.

◇ How Hippos Move

The hippo has short, stubby legs, a barrel-shaped body, and a big heavy head. It doesn't look like a fast runner, but it is. In short bursts, it can gallop more than twenty miles per hour—faster than a human being.

Hippos have webbed toes that help in swimming. But even with all their time in the water, hippos are not very good swimmers. In fact, they do more walking in the water than swimming. They like to be in water that's about five feet deep, which just covers their bodies. Then they walk lightly over the bottom.

Hippos can also dive under the water and stay under for as long as six minutes. Often, they rest there. And they can even walk under water along the river bottom. A hippo's body is dense and heavy. This is what keeps it from floating to the surface.

◇ The Senses of the Hippo

An important thing to note about the eyes, ears, and nostrils of the hippo is that they are placed very high on the head. This allows a hippo to have its whole body and most of its head covered by water and still be on the lookout for danger.

Often that is all you can see of hippos—a bunch of eyes, ears, and snouts sticking up from the water.

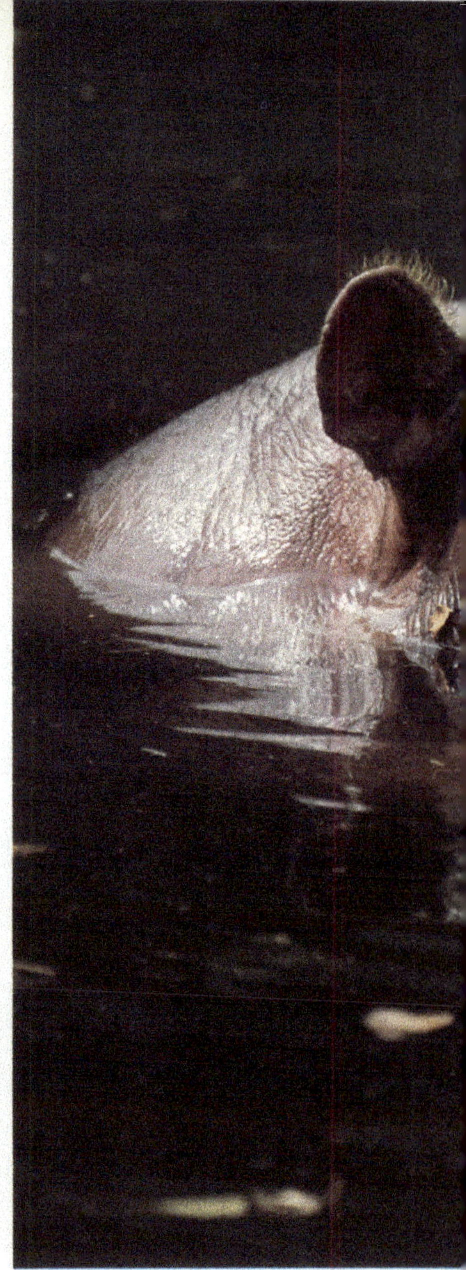

When a hippo dives, it closes its slit-like nostrils until it comes up for air. When it comes up, it opens them. Then it whirls its ears to get the water out.

Hippo skin is thick and tough. Although its body looks hairless, there are some short, fine hairs here and there on the hippo's body and on the tail.

Hippos are most comfortable when in water. When they are out of the water for a while, their skin starts to give off a brownish-

red liquid. It appears in little globs. Because of the reddish color of this liquid, people sometimes say that hippos are "sweating blood." But it's not blood. The liquid is oily. It keeps their skin from getting too dry and acts as a sun-screen. It also may help protect them against infection.

Hippos have good eyesight and can see clearly for about 200 feet. They have good night vision too. When light shines on them, hippos' eyes look red in the dark.

◇ How Hippos Communicate

Hippos often grunt when they see danger approaching. This serves as a warning to the others in the group. But hippos, like many animals, communicate with each other more by actions than by sounds.

For example, when a male hippo opens his mouth very wide, it doesn't mean he is yawning. He is showing his teeth. It is his way of telling another male hippo, "You are coming too close to my territory. Back off—or I'm ready to fight!"

When a baby hippo strays too far from its mother, the mother butts the baby with its head. That way, the baby knows it should come back.

◇ Being Born

Baby hippos are born in the rainy season, when there's lots of grass for the mothers to eat. A good diet means their bodies can make lots of milk for their young.

Although pygmy hippos are born on land, the baby river hippo is born right in the water. It's a big baby, about four feet long

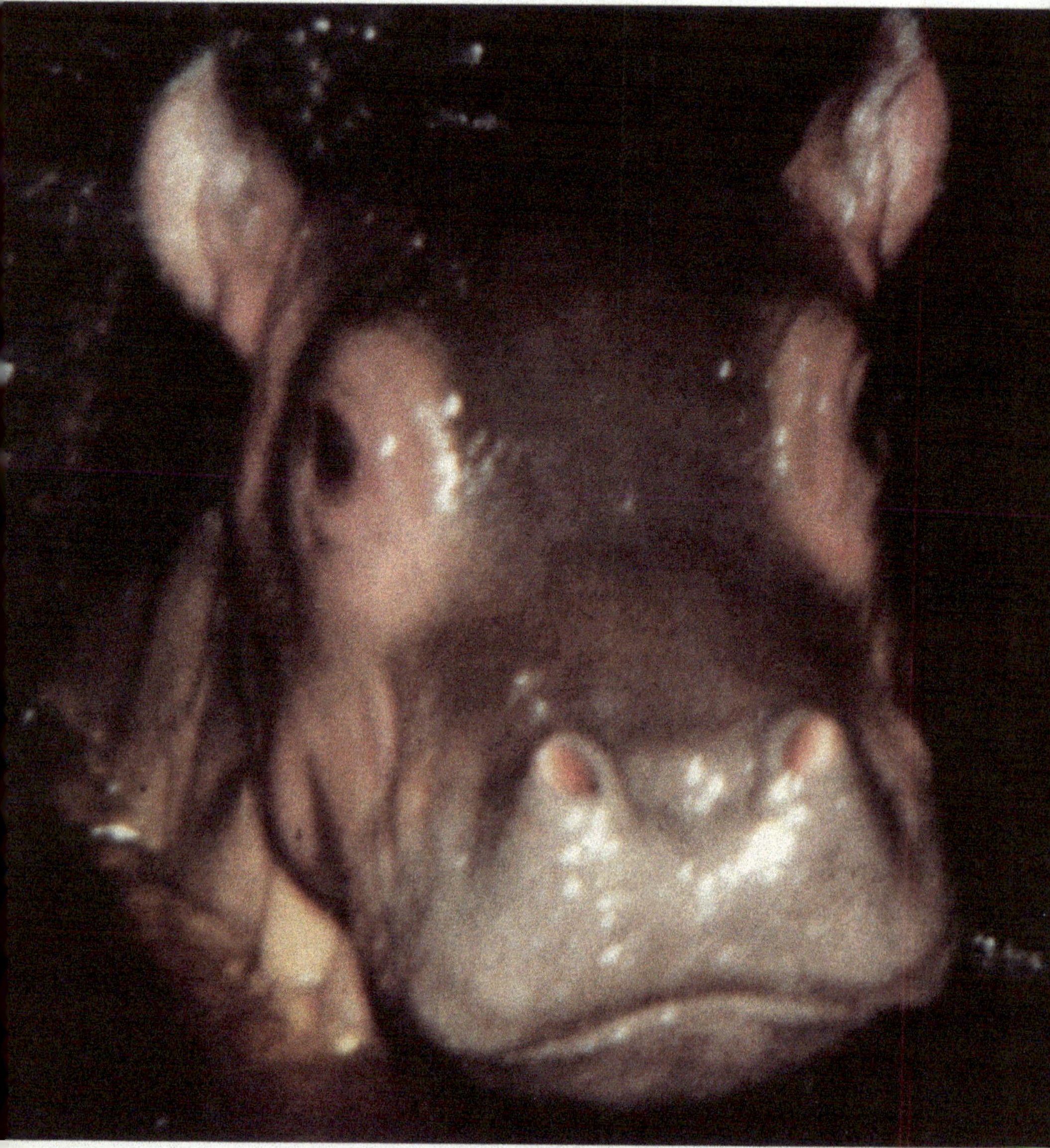

and weighing about 100 pounds. The first thing the newborn hippo does is come to the surface for air.

Water is the safest place for hippos, so that's where the calf and its mother spend most of their time at first. Sometimes, it lies on its mother's back, and rests there while the mother sleeps.

At first, all the mothers with young babies live a bit apart from the other hippos. After about seven weeks they rejoin the larger group.

A baby hippo can walk from its first day, but it's not strong enough to walk far. So, when its mother goes up on land for grass, a young baby stays with the other hippo mothers, who "babysit" until the mother comes back.

◇ Growing Up

As the young hippo gets older, it spends more time on land. The mother hippo protects her young on land as well as in the water. She keeps the baby very close to her, walking on the side closest to any possible danger. On the land, there are lions and leopards, hyenas, and wild dogs. In the water, there are crocodiles. And sometimes, for no reason that scientists understand, an old male hippo, or bull, will rush at a baby hippo and crush it.

By the time the mother and her youngster rejoin the main group of hippos, the young one is able to eat grass and doesn't drink milk any more.

When the youngster is four or five months old, it is no longer endangered by the older male hippos. Often the males play with the young hippos.

The young hippos begin to spend time in groups away from their mothers. This can be a dangerous time, since they are still too small to defend themselves from predators.

By the time a river hippo is a year old, it already weighs more than 500 pounds. It can live up to fifty years.

◇ Living Day to Day

It's quiet on the river. On a sandbar, a group of hippos are napping. A turtle rests on top of one of them. On another, a white bird, a cattle egret, sits pecking. It doesn't seem to bother the hippo as it pecks insects off his skin. Not far off, there are a couple of baby hippos, taking rides on their mothers' backs.

As the sun gets hotter, the hippos slip into the water one by one. All you can see of them now are their backs. They look like big brown mounds. They snooze right in the water. Some disappear altogether and rest underwater. Every three minutes or so, they stick their nostrils up for air. If something disturbs a hippo, there is a swoosh of bubbles. Then its head pops up, blowing out water like a little fountain. Soon it disappears again.

There's no danger around. Some of the hippos begin to eat reeds at the river's edge. It's still very quiet, and it's nice and cool in the water.

Two big bulls stand facing each other in shallow water, their mouths wide open. One has come a little too close to the other's territory.

Suddenly, the two males charge at each other, slashing out with their big, curved teeth. Then one throws himself into the

water, sideways, and escapes. The water is red. He has been wounded.

All the other hippos have moved away from the fighters. Fierce fights are a fact of life in the hippo world, but other hippos are careful not to get in the way. Soon it's quiet again on the river.

In the late afternoon, two lions stroll down to the river to drink. Like submarines, some of the hippos disappear under water. Others grunt in alarm. The lions don't stay long.

As it gets dark, the hippos come up out of the water to eat. But they don't come up on the flat beach where the lions were. They climb up a steep sloping spot at the river's edge. They always leave the river from this same place. Here, the ground has been pounded down hard by the heavy hippos. Sometimes roots and vines grow up and over the path, making the river exit a kind of sunken tunnel.

To get to their grazing areas, the hippos travel along special trails they have created over time. They spend the entire night up on land, eating grass. A hippo can eat 150 pounds of grass in one night.

Here and there along a hippo trail there are huge manure piles, sometimes three feet high. The bull hippos make these piles, which are sometimes called "calling cards." As the bull adds to his pile, he splatters the manure all around with his tail to let the others know he's been by. The females and the young hippos don't do this.

Before daybreak, the hippos are back in the water. Sometimes you can hear them roar as the sun comes up. Then they settle down to another day of snoozing in the water.

◇ Hippos in Captivity

Hippos in zoos live a different kind of life than do hippos in the wild. They are fed in the daytime—not at night. Instead of grass, they eat grain and hay, and they don't eat as much. They still spend a lot of time in the water.

Hippos in the wild are social animals. So if a hippo is alone in a zoo, it often makes friends with other animals. Sometimes the combinations are strange. One hippo in Germany made friends with a dog. The dog would creep partway into the hippo's mouth and lick it.

Another solitary hippo, in the Netherlands, lived next to some elephants. He would lean over the trench that separated them, open his mouth and shake his head. The elephants seemed to understand that he was being friendly. In response they would lean over and stick their trunks or their tails in his mouth. Sometimes the hippo would nibble at their heads.

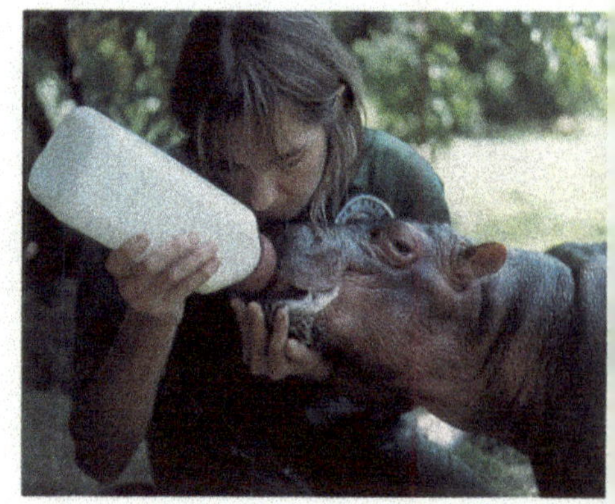

Many hippos in zoos do live with other hippos, though. When there is a male and female pair in a zoo, they often have many babies through the years.

Protecting the Hippos

In the past, tens of thousands of hippos were shot by big-game hunters for "sport." That happens less now, but there is a different threat to hippos today. Bit by bit, more land in the part of the world where hippos live is being developed for use by humans. Wild areas are being turned into villages and farms. The hippos have been losing their habitat—their home.

To help solve this problem, most African countries have set aside large wildlife reserves. These places are not like zoos with cages and shelters. They are wild places where animals can live a normal existence in their natural habitat. People can drive through to watch the animals, but they cannot interfere in their daily lives.

Many hippos today live in these reserves. In central Africa alone there are more than 35,000 hippos, who without these reserves would have a hard time surviving.

About the Contributors

JANE GOODALL was born in London on April 3, 1934, and grew up in Bournemouth, on the southern coast of England. In 1960, she began studying chimpanzees in the wild in Gombe, Tanzania. After receiving her doctorate in ethology at Cambridge University, Dr. Goodall founded the Gombe Stream Research Center for the study of chimpanzees and baboons. In 1977, she established the Jane Goodall Institute for Wildlife Research, Education and Conservation to promote animal research throughout the world. She has written three books for adults, including the bestseller *In the Shadow of Man*, and three books for children, including the recent *My Life With the Chimpanzees* and *The Chimpanzee Family Book*.

MIRIAM SCHLEIN is the author of more than 60 books for children. Six of those have been chosen as Junior Literary Guild selections, six others were named as Outstanding Science Books for Children, as selected by the National Science Teachers Association/Children's Book Council Joint Committee. She is the recipient of the Boys Clubs of America Junior Book Medal, and her book *Project Panda Watch* was cited as an Honor Book by the New York Academy of Sciences. She is the mother of two grown children and lives in New York City.

Jane Goodall's commitment to the animal world is expressed in her words, "Only when we understand can we care. Only when we care can we help. Only when we help shall they be saved." You can learn more about joining in her efforts to protect endangered wildlife by contacting

The Jane Goodall Institute
1120 20th St NW
Washington, DC 20036
Phone: (703) 682-9220

Published by iBooks an imprint of
J. Boylston & Company, Publishers
Produced by Byron Preiss Visual Publications, Inc.
Manhanset House
POB 342
Dering Harbor NY 11965
bricktower@aol.com • www.ibooksinc.com

Interior illustrations by Ralph Reese
Map by Rurick Tyler

Special thanks to Judy Wilson, Jonathan Lanman, Judy Jo
Jan Armstrong, Alan Root, and Bonnie Dalzell.

Editor: Ruth Ashby
Associate Editor: Gwendolyn Smith
Cover design: Ted Mader & Associates
Interior design: Alex Jay/Studio J

Library of Congress Cataloging-in-Publication Data
Schlein, Miriam.
Jane Goodall's animal world. Hippos/by Miriam
Schlein; Alan Root, consultant; photographs by Leona
Lee Rue III and Len Rue, Jr.—
p. cm.
Reprint. Originally published: New York: Athene
1989.
"A Byron Preiss book."
Summary: Introduces the physical characteristics
havior, habitat, reproduction, and life cycle of the hip
ISBN: 978-1-59687-565-4
1. Hippopotamus—Juvenile literature.
[1. Hippopotamus.]
I. Rue, Leonard Lee, ill. II. Rue, Len, ill. III. Titl
QL737.U57S3 1990 599.73'4—dc19 89-6466
CIP AC

www.ingramcontent.com/pod-product-compliance
Lightning Source LLC
Chambersburg PA
CBHW040417110426
42813CB00013B/2679

9781596875654